some of my focus on a new brand I am working on. My team has given much more attention to the details and the practices he outlines in this book.

I am excited for you to experience and apply this content to your business. I look forward to continually having H.B. in my corner with my business.

Chris Lieto: *Ironman Champion.*
Consultant. Coach. Speaker.

Erik Morin

When someone says "sales," usually the Wolf of Wall Street "sell me this pen" will come to mind. Or watching Vin Diesel (in Bowler Room) sell a doctor some stock he knows nothing about. Or the infamous "coffee is for closers" scene from Glengarry Glen Ross. Unfortunately, the marketing and sales industry has adopted some of these same mindsets and tactics that give little attention to the client and the experience the client has.

Potential clients and customers no longer want to be sold. Customers are expecting more, and quite frankly, demanding more from the businesses they work with. Customers want to be associated with companies that have a bigger value than the bottom line for shareholders. H.B has created the Ideal Client Experience (ICX) with this in mind. He has flipped the outdate "sales funnel" concept on its head and created a step-by-step guide on how to turn prospects into clients and then into advocates.

What I respect most about H.B is the grace and understanding he gives to the owners he works with. He understands that there is always a fire to put out, and yet he challenges his to clients to slow down and visualize the bigger picture. His uncanny ability to lead you so that you come up with your own answer is one of his best gifts (as with any great coach).

ICX is a great roadmap for any business that wants to go to the next level. I am confident that this book will do the same for you, and I encourage you to absorb the information in the spirit with which H.B wrote it: with an open mind, a willingness to grow, and the curiosity to find a more rewarding way to work with current clients and to attract new ones.

Erik Morin: Advisor.
Financial Problem Solver for Business Owners

THE BIG IDEA

As you already know:

Successful business is no longer dominated by those who have the best price. The low price leaders are huge and rare. It is important for all mid and small business owners to know: *if you want to lose marketshare, then you should try to compete on providing the lowest price (Corp-Intl).*

You may also know that offering the best product does not guarantee success. *Even if people love your company or product, in the U.S. 59% will walk away after several bad experiences (PWC).* The modern consumer has other issues that are pulling ahead of quality as the winning play.

The best businesses in the world now compete on a new field. There is a new sport for gaining customers and increasing revenue. This contest is fought over one thing: best customer experience. *Back in 2020, 77% of consumers considered CX [Client Experience] just as important as the*

*quality of products and services (Forbes), and now client
experience is beating both price and product on the field of
business competition, by a wide margin (Walker).*

Will the *Ideal Client Experience* really save your
business? Only if your business requires customers. *83% of
200 surveyed executives said unimproved client experience is
putting their revenue and market share at risk (Forbes Insights
and Arm Treasure Data survey).*

Will the Ideal Client Experience really save your business?

Only if your business requires customers.

Or clients.

Or investors.

Or donors.

I do not need to ask:

Do you want to grow your business?

Of course you do. I am asking a better question. A *how* question. How do you think your business will create sustainable growth in the season ahead? There have been many voices trying to answer this question for you in many different ways. But the market has changed. The answer has evolved.

Way back in 2012 more than 66% of companies were competing primarily on the basis of customer experience – up from only 36% in the year before (SuperOffice). This insight marks a significant shift in the modern marketplace that will continue into the future. Apparently, the amount of quick-access information on *best price* and *best product* is no longer enough to drive growth. Delivering information is no longer enough to attract and maintain new customers. You may have to deliver something else.

The old adage is coming true in a new way, "People won't remember what you said. They will remember how you made them feel."

People won't remember what you said.

They will remember
how you made them feel.

It is time for you to consider how you make your customers, your clients, your investors, and your donors ... feel.

Maybe you think I was being melodramatic when I used the title, "How the Ideal Client Experience Will Save Your Business." I could have expressed it more gently by writing, "How the *Ideal Client Experience* Will Grow Your Business." I was trying to get your attention. It is time to take note and get moving. If you don't, you will get left behind. *There is a pressing strategic imperative for brands to compete on customer experience (CX) in nearly every industry. Consumers have spoken on what's most important to them in a modern customer experience; privacy, consistency across multiple channels, a deep understanding – and appreciation – of customer needs, and personalization. (RedPointGlobal)*

With that in mind, here are four practical ways the *Ideal Client Experience* will actually save your business:

1. Client Retention

It will improve customer retention. What costs your business more time, money and effort—keeping your present customers or winning new ones? *You may already know that it costs five times as much to acquire new customers than it does to keep current ones (Forrest).*

2. Team Culture

The *Ideal Client Experience* will boost team culture. More

than ever, people choose to stay engaged in jobs they feel are making a difference. They also want to make a difference while working alongside people they enjoy. What costs you more time, money, and effort—retaining present team members or hiring and onboarding new ones? *It may cost up to 150% of a technical employees salary to replace them (PeopleKeep). And research also shows 70% of employees say having a friend at work is critical (OfficeVibe).* Treating team-members and customers to an excellent experience develops a more attractive company for everyone.

3. Client Loyalty

The *Ideal Client Experience* will create loyal clients. If the first two reasons were phrased from a cost saving point of view, let's look at this last reason from a positive angle. What grows revenue in your company faster —repeat client loyalty or securing and selling to new clients you haven't met? The data shows *average companies tend to lose 50% of their customers in 5 years and 50% of their employees in 4 years (The Loyalty Effect, Reichheld).* What do you think even a slight improvement in client loyalty would do for your revenue?

4. Client Advocacy

Let's ask another question related to your present clients. What would help you secure better clients—your best clients advocating for you among their peers, or a marketing team promoting you to strangers? Even when beginning new marketing campaigns to increase sales, *businesses are three times more likely to sell a product to an existing customer than to a new prospect (Marketing Metrics), and ahead of all other trust metrics, 83% say they completely or somewhat trust the recommendations of friends and family (Nielsen).*

You are sitting on a goldmine.

Many have treated client experience like an add-on. It may seem like something that only very empathetic people can do. It may seem like a luxury expense for those who have loads of extra time. However, this kind of antiquated thinking can cause you to leave boatloads of cash on the table. *Differentiated customer experience will bring in 5.7 times more revenue than companies that fail to act on it. (Forrester)*

Seriously? 5.7 times? Honestly, that sounds exaggerated.

Most business owners will just work harder if they hit a slow down in growth. They might return to more aggressive sales techniques. However, a sales-at-any-cost mindset is not worth it. Heavy-handed salesmanship creates downward drag inside of bad customer experience. It can leave a wake of disenfranchisement. This is costly to repair, and this mindset will have you running on a hamster wheel of fatigue. It makes me tired thinking about it.

For many, internet-based marketing feels like a money pit. It seems like a fixer upper that takes but never gives. Hiring digital agencies and social media experts, as well as inventing and deploying new ad strategies, really adds up. But where is the measurable growth from these dollars? This stuff is supposed to work, so we just keep spending in the hope of overtaking the cost-benefit curve at some point in the future. Can we really compete with digital giants?

Please don't misunderstand. I would not encourage you to abandon any useful sales training or internet marketing tool that is producing results. But I would encourage you to think about the ROI from your recent efforts. Like the man in Texas said after spitting chewing tobacco on the fence post, "How's that working out for ya?"

Maybe we should flip the script.

Let's play to your strength.

You are sitting on a goldmine.

I am here to affirm what you already know. Right in the center of your present business is the secret to your long-term sustainable success. Smack in the happy place of your present client base is a growth machine that can't be stopped: *your ideal clients!* These ideal clients are an untapped nuclear power source for your most profitable growth. They already bring you joy and profit. So, what if you had more of them and less of everyone else? If that rings a bell, then you have a reason to read on.

In just a few pages I will show you how to create an ideal experience for your ideal clients.

This will transform your best clients into your best advocates.

This will lead to the right kind of growth for your company because these wonderful customers will reproduce after their own kind.

Never drop the ball again.

This is a team sport and we all need to develop better ball-handling skills. Everyone on the team must work together to win in the game of client experience. The worst thing we could do is keep dropping the ball and losing clients we have worked so hard to win.

Client experience affects our hearts because we care for the people we serve. This means every bit of effort you put into creating an excellent client experience is going to bring you and your team more peace and more joy.

If moving the ball forward every day, every week, is important to your business, then I challenge you to take the first step toward winning in client experience. I will show you how to take that first step (and a few more). I will help you put an *Ideal Client Experience* plan into action so your team will never drop the ball again.

HELPFUL HARDWARE

A short story.

Let me share a short story about the rewards of developing the *Ideal Client Experience*. I want to illustrate some key ideas by using an oversimplified story–a business fable–so you can easily extract insights for your industry.

Maybe?

Howard's butt crack was sticking out from under the kitchen sink as he tried with determination to accomplish his home improvement task. Tools, bottles, brushes, and stuff from the cabinet had exploded onto the floor all around him. His wife stood in the kitchen with her hands on her hips and said, "I told you that we should have just called a plumber. Now what?"

Unable to breathe and hurting from the twisted up position he found himself in, Howard slid onto the floor, rolled over, looked up, grunted, and stretched out his hand to show the dirty little part he had extracted from under the sink. He held it up like a prize.

"This is it," he said proudly. "All I have to do is find a new one of these thing-a-ma-jigs. I'll have to look for the nearest hardware store."

Pearl and Howard had just moved to town and didn't know the neighborhood at all. Pearl picked up a door-hanger that had missed the trashcan on an earlier attempt to throw it away. She said, "I just found this flyer on the front door advertising a hardware store, and it says they are only five minutes away."

The flyer's bold type section read:

New to town? Moving can be hard. Let us help! We are right around the corner! Helpful Hardware.

Meet

It was starting to sprinkle when Howard arrived in the Helpful Hardware parking lot. As he pulled in, he braced himself for a frustrating experience. He had never had a pleasant experience at the hardware store in the town they just moved from. It never had what he needed. They had stuff that was close but never the thing he actually needed. What's worse is that they never seemed to care. He usually entered and exited alone because the staff seemed to be hiding in the back.

As he circled one parking row near the door, he saw a big A-frame sign in the middle of the sidewalk at the front doors of the store. It was bright red and had huge, bold, white letters that read:

We have what you are looking for!

Discover

When Howard walked through the automatic sliding doors, he was greeted by a welcome air-conditioning blast and a smiling face. The lady behind the face asked, "What are you working on today?"

He found it strange that she didn't ask, "What can I help you find?" He repeated her words in his mind:

What are you working on today?

As this mental machinery was working itself through his brain, he realized he was relieved that she hadn't asked about the item. The fact was that he didn't know the name of the dirty thing-a-ma-jig he was holding in his hand. So he just blurted out, "I was under the sink working on the garbage disposal and this thing was obviously broken."

She nodded in affirmation, as though she had seen this thing before, and pointed to the back right corner of the store.

"Let's go back to plumbing together. I think we have

that exact part. But if we don't have what you need today, we will work to make it right. My name is Sammie. What's yours?"

As he replied, Howard's blood pressure dropped by several points, and he followed her deeper into the store.

Design

Staring at a wall of plumbing parts created the same amount of frustration as a one-hundred item restaurant menu—there were too many items to understand where to begin.

> *"There is usually more than one way to do this repair,"*

Sammie said, breaking Howard's trance. "Look. Up here are the kits where you can replace the entire assembly all at one time. And, down here are the individual parts you can purchase one at at time. So, tell me, is the garbage disposal more than a few years old?"

"Honestly, I don't know," he replied.

"Well, you could start by replacing this single part." She pulled the part from the wall and handed it to him. "And if it leaks again, just come back and get a whole new assembly." She paused to allow him a little processing time, and then followed up with,

"What would you prefer to do?"

Howard thought about her question and replied, "I have other stuff I want to accomplish today, so the fast-fix is what I want. Let me just buy the part."

Implement

Sammie, getting ready to return to the front of the store, handed Howard a business card and said, "Here is my card. If you need help with anything, just call or text me—it is my work cell. If you're in the store and I don't pick up right away, just push the call button on the end of the aisle. It turns on that light up there over your head so we know where you are. Hey, don't forget to let me know how it went, OK?"

He looked down at the card.

We are always here when you need us.
Helpful Hardware.

Sammie's name and a cell phone number were on the card, too. He realized in a flash that he had no fear of *separation anxiety.* That was what he called it when he was left alone after a decision like this, especially if someone had given advice and then mysteriously disappeared. He grunted his approval in the style of Tim Allen, smiled, stuffed the card in his pocket and started his journey toward the front of the store.

Deliver

Howard was passing several aisles along the way that smelled of different projects. There was the rubber O-ring smell on the fasteners aisle, and then he noticed the insecticide and lawn stuff smell. Howard did not like lawn work so he frowned as he walked by. Right when he passed the oily, metallic smell of the key-making machine, he saw a customer in the checkout line who had a cart full of random stuff that was piled up in a gigantic mound. He knew that this was going to take forever. He was about to say it aloud when a young man carrying a hand-held scanning device approached him. He announced, "If you are ready, I can check you out right here."

No lines? Amazing!

The young man with the name tag that read *Client Care Leader* asked, "What is your name?"

"Howard Riley."

He punched it in to the device. Then he scanned his item and scanned his credit card. As he was finishing, he asked, "Can I get your email address for the receipt?"

"Sure."

"Can I get your phone number for customer service use only, never for sales calls?"

"OK."

"If you ever come in and can't find what you are looking for, just go to Larry at that counter over there. If we don't have it, Larry will call around and try to find it for you—same day—so you don't lose any time on your project."

Larry was standing inside a four-sided island in the center of the store with a computer to his side and a bunch of odd things scattered across the counters. Above him was a sign that read:

Let's Find What You Need, TODAY!

Hmm.

When the warm outside air hit him, he realized he had just done what he usually refused to do: he had actually shared his contact information with a retail store.

What was I thinking?

He un-squinched his face, dropped his shoulders, and said aloud, "Well, they seem like a pretty smart bunch."

The sun was out, the pavement was steaming, and humidity was transforming the air into hot pudding.

Affinity

By the time the air conditioning kicked on in the car and just before he put the car in gear, his phone dinged. He checked it to make sure it wasn't Pearl with one of her famous last-minute requests that would require him to get out and go back into the store. The text was from a new number, and it read:

> *Hi neighbor! We loved helping you today. Is there anything we could improve to make your next visit even better? Helpful Hardware.*

He grunted. This time his eyebrows went up. It was odd, but it was a pleasant surprise. He typed, "Nope. Today was great. Thanks."

Immediately the text auto-reply came back:

> *You are part of our community, and without your feedback we can't become better friends. Thank you!*

And then one more text appeared:

> *Please opt-in to our LOCALS ONLY monthly email so we can send you VIP discounts and invitations to special events.*

Advocacy

"Pearl, you won't believe how easy that was," he announced as he was setting his keys and phone on the only clean space he could find in the entry area. He had to step over some boxes in the living room as he kept talking. "You also won't believe it, but I only had to go to one store to find that thing-a-ma-jig for the sink repair. I love our new hardware."

Just as he entered the kitchen where Pearl had been cleaning up after his earlier mess-making, his phone dinged a different ding. It was his email app, and there was an email from the Helpful Hardware address. He held up the phone to Pearl and said, "They already asked me how they could improve their service before I was even out of the parking lot." He turned the phone back to himself and read the high points.

> *What was your favorite part about visiting with us today?*
>
> ◎ *Smart service*
>
> ◎ *Same-day guarantee*
>
> ◎ *Fast checkout*
>
> ◎ *Making friends*
>
> ◎ *Other*
>
> *Glad you are part of our neighborhood!*
> *You help us make it a better place. Sammie*

He made his choice and smashed his finger on the "Smart Service" tick-box to leave the feedback and grunted again. He said aloud, "Seriously friendly."

There were some sales coupons in the email. There was a note about the free Saturday workshop, too. It was that last sentence, however, that really meant something to him.

Glad you are part of the neighborhood!

He kept thinking about it as he finished up the repair under the sink. When he finally stood up, he saw potato chips on the counter. Without hesitation, he shoved some into his mouth.

The move had been hard. It was hard on Howard and Pearl, but it was also hard on the friends they had to leave behind. He was just beginning to understand why moving was on the top ten list of the most stressful events in life as he made his way through the maze of boxes out to the garage.

For the first time since the moving truck had pulled away from his old neighborhood, Howard felt his shoulders relax just a little. He felt like he belonged here, in this place, just a bit more.

He sat in the lawn chair and fished through the cooler full of cold miracles. As he cracked the can, he imagined the free workshop at the hardware next weekend.

THE EIGHT STEPS

Do you remember them?

In our story, we learned how one business proactively engaged their customers along each step of the client experience. As you could see, Helpful Hardware had taken time to carefully craft the interactions that would happen at every step. There were eight steps. Do you remember them?

#1

Maybe?

The moment a future customer realizes that we might be the answer to his or her specific problem.

#2

Our very first chance to shake hands, virtually or in person, with the customer.

#3

Discover

The place where both business and customer dive in and learn about each other, personally and professionally.

#4

A time to share strategic wisdom and give the customer
the power to choose.

#5

Implement

This is when we follow through on our value proposition
and get it done.

Deliver

The singular moment of celebrating the completion of our
promise to the customer.

#7

Affinity

Resetting the business-client relationship to create long-term loyalty.

#8

Advocacy

The magical season where clients naturally advocate for
us—first to themselves and then to others.

THE ICX FRAMEWORK

The first line in the diagram.

I see everything in pictures. Turn the page and see the eight steps of the client experience journey. You will recognize the arc in the middle of the diagram because it looks like a traditional sales pipeline.

This line represents the

PURPOSE of your business.

DISCOVER   DESIG

MAYBE?   MEET

The client's journey starts here.

...MPLEMENT DELIVER

AFFINITY ADVOCACY

Newsflash: So far we have been speaking about these steps from our point of view. However, a more strategic way to look at the client relationship is to pivot and get into the client's shoes. We need to see all eight steps from their point of view. Say these next two sentences aloud:

Our point of view doesn't matter.

All that matters is the client's point of view.

QUESTIONS & ANSWERS

We need a system.

If we want to win the game of client experience and amaze our ideal clients, we will need to build a system designed just for them. It will need to work for our whole team, and then our whole team will need to focus entirely on these measurable outcomes. We can't depend on a few members of our team who are naturally empathetic. Even those of us who are more analytical should be able to participate. We don't all have to be empathetic savants if we have a practical client-care system that empowers everyone on our team to participate. This is what it looks like when we distill questions for every step of the client journey. Turn the page:

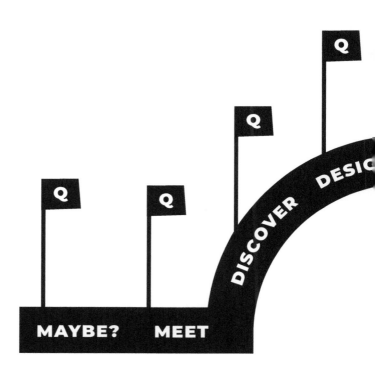

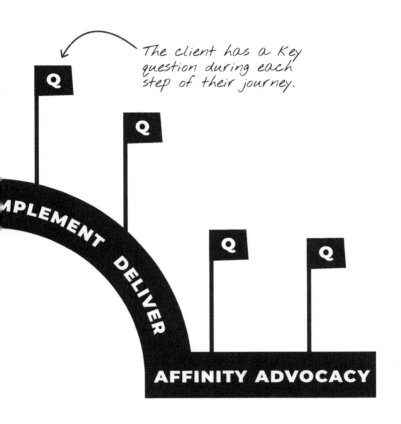

The client has a key question during each step of their journey.

SYSTEMATIZE EMPATHY

That is what we are going to do.

Let's see how Helpful Hardware turned empathy into a system. They distilled the client's primary questions through every step of the client experience. They also determined their best answer for each question. Here is how:

1. Maybe?

After a solid review of recent customer data, Helpful Hardware concluded that the key to their long-term success was repeat customers. The ROI was much, much better over time. However, if they didn't capture new customers as soon as they moved to town, they were going to be just one more hardware on the list of many. They determined the most important question new residents would be asking—right at the moment of first opportunity—was simply:

What hardware is closest to me?

Helpful Hardware's customer base lived within a fifteen mile radius from their store, but there were three other hardware stores within reach. Since anyone moving to town was likely to open their phone and find the nearest hardware store on a map, Helpful Hardware decided to step in front of the web search by placing door hangers on every house within fifteen miles that was for sale or any house that had recently sold. This would let them answer the client's question before they even asked it.

We are very close and we care about you.

2. Meet

In their weekly meetings, the whole team started wearing caps that read, "Customer." They would wear them and brainstorm as if they were in their best customer's shoes. They tried to think like them. They realized their best customers were not looking for just best price or best product. They distilled their best customer's feelings down to one issue:

I wonder if they have what I am looking for?

Every hardware has signs out on the sidewalk announcing seasonal sales, but the leadership team decided to rock the boat and do something radically different. They transformed all of the storefront signage to answer the one question they knew their customers were asking when they first met:

We have what you are looking for.

3. Discover

The leadership team at Helpful Hardware loved solving problems. Most of the team had experience in the trades; however, when they wore their "Customer" caps, they thought completely differently. They thought like their neighbors who had just run into a problem at home. This meant their visiting customers all had one common feeling as they engaged the team.

Will they understand my problem?

(And maybe, in addition: "Will they make me feel stupid since I may not understand the problem?")

Helpful Hardware revamped their training manual for all retail employees. They no longer called anyone a *Sales Associate*. They now call them *Client Care Leaders*. This move required a new script for engaging every customer who entered the store. They wrote out the script step by step. The driving force behind the script was something they would say aloud in their team meetings every week: I will discover each customer's goals because I am genuinely interested. This created their simple answer:

We want to understand your goals and treat you with respect.

4. Design

Most people could search for how-to videos for any household project. The team concluded, however, that some problems were best solved by talking to real people. Salesmanship was not only useless, it was annoying. Respectful counsel was the true value of a trip to Helpful Hardware. At this stage of customer experience their best local clients would be asking:

Will they educate and help me make a good choice?

The primary job, then, for every Client Care Leader could be wrapped up in one statement: I will design solutions because I care about the outcome, and I care about it today. This commitment led to all kinds of new contributions from team members. They worked on how to gracefully design solutions instead of just selling products. And they emphasized same-day solutions.

I will show you solutions or I will find someone who can, today.

5. Implement

The leadership team was absolutely sure the most difficult customer care problem was separation anxiety. This was specifically true for those who were having things repaired at the service counter. To help the whole team understand it, they used role-play as a learning exercise. They talked about how it felt to be forgotten. They recounted their own customer experiences. They began to empathize with clients who felt lost when they didn't understand the process. So, for both repair customers and in-store shoppers, the team distilled their key customer question down to:

Will I get support after I buy, or will I be all alone?

The team decided on two distinct answers to the problem of separation anxiety. The first was to buy every *Client Care Leader* a company cell phone. The number was placed on their own personal business cards. The phone system never put a customer on hold, never played a robot voice, and always connected to a real person day or night. They hired a third party answering service to deliver on this commitment even after hours. The second answer was in the form of help lights installed at the end of every aisle. They were very bright and easy to see. Everyone knew to move quickly, help the customer, and get that light turned off.

We make customer service personal and we make it fast.

6. Deliver

In retail sales, delivery is really a question of speed. When the line in front of us at the checkout gets too long, we start deciding if what we have in our cart is really worth the wait. Some of us would drop our stuff and just walk out. At the very least, we regret the whole experience because it ended poorly. The team decided to post this question as most important during the delivery phase of client experience:

> *Can I get it today and can I get out of here quickly?*

The leadership team knew their store size would not allow them to stock everything for everyone. Sending people to the internet was definitely not the answer. They innovated. First, they focused their in-store inventory around the most common residential projects. Second, they prioritized speed of service. If they didn't have the item in stock, the *Project Specialist Team* would call other hardware stores in the area until they found the part. They would then ask the other store to hold it as they sent the customer directly to them. They were becoming famous among many other store owners in the area. They delivered the answer every customer wanted to hear:

> *If we don't have it, we will find it for you today, in town.*

7. Affinity

The very core of Helpful Hardware's mission was building client loyalty. It made more efficient money year after year than anything else. They believed their best clients viewed them as neighbors, not as a warehouse. Their clients wanted to feel as if they were old friends. After another role-play workshop, the team concluded that these customers were asking one fundamental question:

Who am I to them?

Helpful Hardware wanted to connect with customers as friends. They wanted to connect as neighbors who cared for their community. This would build valuable client loyalty. They decided to use surveys that treated the customers as experts. They asked for customer feedback. They implemented upgrades and made sure their clients knew it. This is how they responded to the customer's question:

Your feedback will help us become a better hardware store, and better neighbors, too.

8. Advocacy

Creating customer advocates is a high goal for any successful business. It is the last step in the *Ideal Client Experience*. For Helpful Hardware, they decided to keep it simple. They first wanted their best customers to advocate for themselves. They wanted each customer to be able to

*Map your client experience
on this 8-step empathy map.*

PURPOSE

Client experience is your purpose.

This is the very first step in building a great client experience. Get your team together and brainstorm. This is a team sport. Take your cues from Helpful Hardware. Can you distill your customer's most important questions down to one key feeling in each step? If you need to, change the word customer to client. Or donor. Or investor. Make it work for you.

Do not slow down. Put on your own "Customer" caps and brainstorm through all eight steps. The main line we have drawn in our ICX diagram represents your firm's PURPOSE. Do not bog down on small details. Do not argue over nuance. Think basic. Get it done. Post it for everyone to see.

Turn the page and see what happens when we add our answers to the client questions.

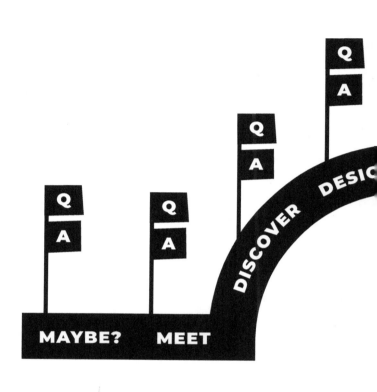

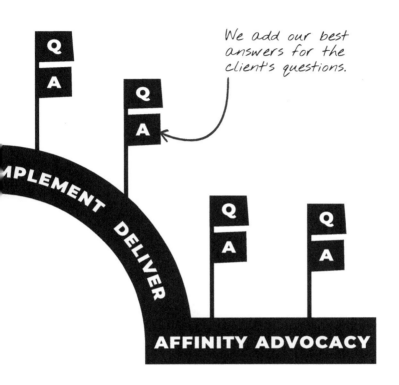

PROCESS

A process for every step.

It was not enough for Helpful Hardware to just map the client questions. It was not enough to create thoughtful answers. They had to put their company to work actually supplying these answers as quickly as they could. This is where empathy becomes practical. This is where you can create a *business playbook* that will guide your new operating system.

When you succeed in implementing an Ideal Client Experience, you will generate a powerful *advocacy arc.* You will see it on the next page.

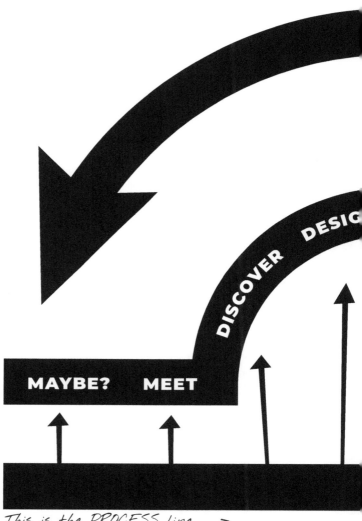

MAYBE?   MEET   DISCOVER   DESIG

This is the PROCESS line. →

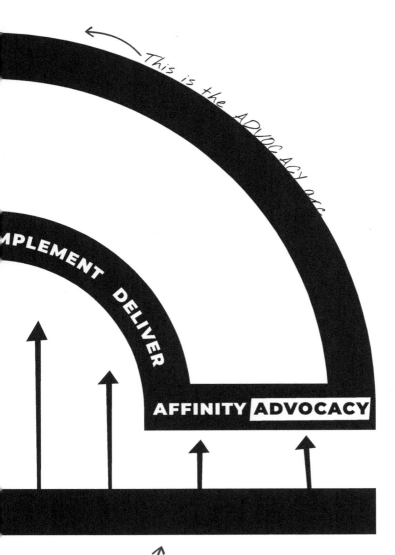

This is the ADVOCACY arc

IMPLEMENT DELIVER

AFFINITY **ADVOCACY**

PROCESS tools
support every
step in the
client experience.

We must identify every single tool and process that supports each step of the client experience. This is accomplished step by step. You already know what many of these tools are. Some tools on this line are technical. Some are personal talents. Some are obvious. Some are more sophisticated. These process tools will have only one purpose:

Answer the client's questions while delivering your value.

It's your turn. Use this QR code and download the client journey map. Fill in the most important process tools you must use to deliver your answers to your clients along the *Ideal Client Experience.*

This worksheet adds process tools to your client experience map.

PEOPLE

A person for every process.

Now, it is time to put our treasure to work. What is our real treasure? The people on our team!

Every person on our team must identify how they will contribute to the process that supports our *Ideal Client Experience*. In our diagram, the line at the bottom represents the people who will lead and support every process. This is how it looks when we add the last line to our framework:

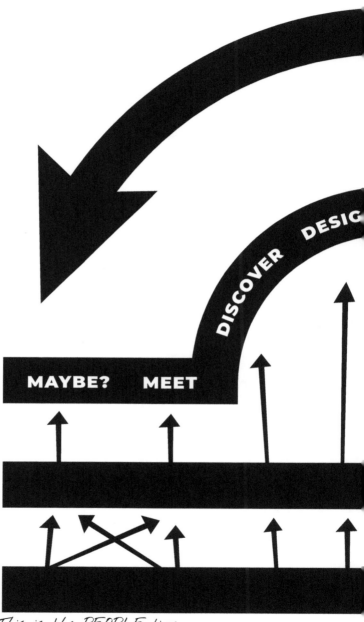

MAYBE? MEET

DISCOVER DESIG

This is the PEOPLE line.

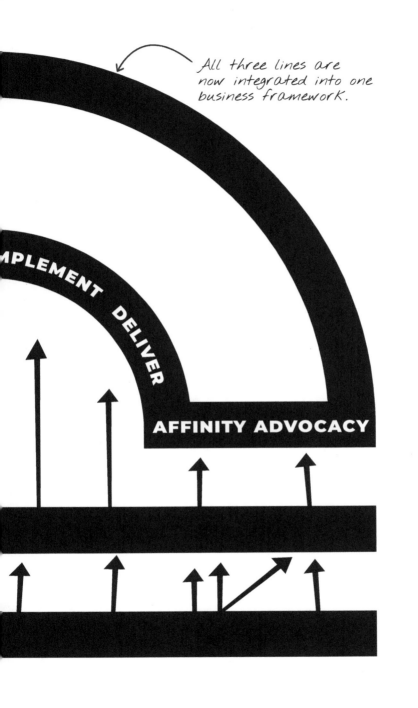

We must associate a person with every client experience tool. There must be a PERSON leading every step in our PROCESS. When we do this, we will discover some gaps. We will also find some overlaps.

Download the PDF version of this full sized mapping exercise and find out who will lead every process.

This worksheet will help you identify your team member roles.

The summary diagram.

Now, let's summarize the *Ideal Client Experience* map in a single graphic. Turn the page, and you will see the diagram you first saw on the outside of the book. It will all make sense. You will never forget it. This is a simple summary of all the work we have accomplished.

It is the ICX framework.

It is your new business playbook.

Remember, every business is built on these three key elements:

Purpose, Process, and People.

These three integrated elements are pictured in the ICX framework. Every successful business will harmonize them so they work together. They will build process tools to serve their primary purpose: client experience. They will cultivate the people who support the overall client journey. They will fearlessly remove anything and anyone who fails to make solid contributions.

The issue in every smart business idea is not in coming up with the idea. It is certainly not in designing a smart diagram. It is in getting it done. I know what happens in moments like this. I know because it happens to me. I see the mountain I need to climb. I know what the big steps are along the journey, but the whole thing seems overwhelming. I don't know where to begin. I don't know if I can sustain the effort. I don't know if I can get the team on board. I don't want to start talking about another great idea and not be able to follow through to completion.

I hear you.

Turn the page and let's take the first steps together.

ACTION PLAN

Three simple steps.

Here are three practical steps to help you make progress today and keep moving until you cross the finish line.

Step one: Stop the bleeding.

This is an exercise that will take one team meeting—no more than one hour. There are four things to accomplish:

First, post the work you have already done with your team on developing your ICX playbook. Don't worry about perfection. The first draft is powerful. It can be revised later. Not now. Make the framework big so everyone can see. Use the entire whiteboard. Get your team to use the markers. Keep it simple.

If you love to see things in lists, use the document behind the QR code to review your client experience map in a different way:

Review and improve your
client experience right now.

Second, circle the steps in the client journey where your team is doing a solid job. Take a moment and be thankful for the steps where your team is already doing a great job. Celebrate your team! Call them out. There is a good chance these strong steps are where your genius and your team's natural talents are shining. Smile. Congratulate.

Third, circle the steps of the client journey where you know your clients are not as happy. You must be brutally honest and listen to your teammates. Where are you losing people? Where are the people or the tools just not getting the job done?

Lastly, in this meeting, without further discussion on the other stuff, brainstorm ways to fill in that gap. Focus only on the worst danger zone. What can you do this week, this month, to better serve your client experience in this trouble spot? Identify it. Write it down. Define the action steps with your team. Take volunteers to lead. Assign responsibilities. Now, announce to the team: *We are going to get this done in the next 30 days.*

Step two: Stop incentivizing work.

Every great business runs on more than one person's genius. Your team must come along with you. In order to rebuild your business systems around supporting an *Ideal Client Experience*, everyone has to be on board. This means you must *stop incentivizing work.*

We all know that we get what we pay for. What we reward, we will get more of. If you pay people to do a job, they will do the job. If you incentivize them to do it harder, better, faster, then they will do it harder, better, faster.

And this is exactly where many businesses hamstring their own success.

I am sorry to have to tell you, but you could be the problem. You have been asking people to do their job and rewarding them for doing it, and that is all you have received. You got what you paid for.

What if you rewarded your team for taking care of the customer's questions and providing your best answers along the way? What if you incentivized the *Ideal Client Experience?* Research shows *42% of customers would pay more for a friendly, welcoming experience. And, among U.S. customers, 65% find a positive experience with a brand to be more influential than great advertising (PWC).*

It is time to start incentivizing client experience.

It is time to reward empathy in action.

Along these lines, Helpful Hardware started trying some new things to create better client experience leadership. I bet some of these examples will prompt some new ideas for your team:

In the *Maybe?* stage of client experience, they stopped paying the marketing firm for Facebook ads targeting the whole city, and they started paying an employee to place new door hangers on every home for sale or homes recently sold within a fifteen mile radius. The employee did online research for homes on the market using real estate search engines (free), printed the hangers locally (designed by an excellent local firm), and personally delivered them every Friday so that weekend warriors had them in hand on Saturday morning. This employee was not paid by the hour. Her or she was paid per door hanger delivered. *The lesson:* Stop paying anyone, including third party services, for hourly work. Start paying them for outcomes. Reward the activities that will deliver great experience to your clients.

Weekly cash bonuses were established in the *Discovery* stage of the client journey. A *Customer Care Leader* had to hand a card to a customer and record the customer's name and the kind of project they were working on. It was only a very small bonus per win, but over a week, it really added up. These simple rewards created deeper discovery, better team culture, and healthier client interaction. *The lesson:* Employees do what they are incentivized to do. If you pay for busy work, people will stay busy. If you celebrate activities that provide great client experience, you will get great client experience.

Another weekly accolade was launched to reward Larry and the whole *Project Specialist Team* for their work during *Implementation.* Any week they scored a 90% success rate on providing same-day solutions for the customers, they were treated to a free lunch from the local pizza joint. After any six consecutive weeks, every *Project Specialist Team* member received a memorable cash bonus. This had all of them working hard to find ways to answer client needs locally and on the same day. Their new goal was never to allow a customer to walk out of the store without a same-day answer to his or her problem. *The lesson:* Culture beats strategy every time. Rewards, accolades, and incentives build great culture. And great culture is the outcome for great people who are focused on doing great things together. Celebrate what you want to create.

Just in case we bogged down in these examples, here is the summary of this simple action step: Plan a meeting with your leadership team and come up with ways to reward one another for improving the first client experience danger zone. Set some new bonuses and reward programs for other areas of your client experience journey where there is not enough leadership.

You get what you pay for.

Announce to the whole team: *Your success will be rewarded at the end of this 30-day period.*

Step three: Stop thinking.

The plan you are putting in motion is addressing one ongoing question: *How do we help our customers experience us as a trustworthy value from start to finish?* This must not become just another great idea. You must conquer this question one bit at a time. It is time to stop thinking and start doing.

Every great business idea has to come down out of the heavens and find a practical implementation on the ground. This is how we make progress. Move the ball every day.

Every week.

Every month.

Over time, your client experience will become world class—but you have to start small.

Make small and repeat.

If there is more than one danger zone on your client experience map, don't panic. Thinking about all of them at one time can be overwhelming. Trying to do too much at one time will crush your team and kill your ability to keep making progress. Purposely put off tackling the next trouble spot until next month. And, above all, do not let this become academic. Make it practical and make it repeatable. Don't think. Do.

Step four: Repeat.

Next month in your review meeting, you will have four basic items on the agenda:

1. Reward Successes.
2. Review Obstacles.
3. Revise the Plan.
4. Repeat the 30-Day Attack.

NEVER DROP THE BALL AGAIN

Hey, author, get to the point.

Did you jump to the end to read the summary? I don't blame you. *Hey, business author, just get to the point already!* Here is the point of the whole book:

> ### *The Ideal Client Experience will literally save your business.*

The body of this book underlined why the *Ideal Client Experience* is mission critical for your business growth. We also went step-by-step through all eight *Ideal Client Experience* steps in the Helpful Hardware business fable. By extracting insights from this overly simplified example, you have discovered how to improve and implement an *Ideal*

Client Experience in your business. This short read has helped you create a customer-driven business playbook.

I worked for decades in the nonprofit world. Nonprofit organizations are not looking for donors: they need lifetime donors. Otherwise, they are consigned to chasing one-off donations from a sea of strangers. Not worth it.

I also worked for decades as a professional artist. I wrote hundreds of songs, published dozens of books and albums, and I gained millions of listeners over time. However, my success was not built on selling my creative work to an ocean of strangers. I achieved that success by building trusting relationships with hundreds of key leaders and pioneers. This is why I was able to book over 125 concerts a year for most of the 90s and produce over seven million song streams on Spotify alone.

More recently I have worked with financial service professionals focusing on growing their businesses. Their client experience journey is anything but short. As it turns out, financial advisors seek loyal, lifelong clients as well. All financial advisors know to abide by the KYC (Know Your Client) rule as a baseline for good practice. The *Ideal Client Experience*, however, moves this expectation up to the KYCQ rule: *Know Your Client's Questions.* This additional level of relational intelligence makes all the difference when trust-building is the key to long term success.

One of my favorite clients in the last year was a real estate developer. She, too, needed to develop a client experience that would create lifetime investors. Implementing the *Ideal Client Experience* was the key to attracting better investors and reaching her multi-million dollar funding goal at a record-setting pace.

Whether your client experience travels for a few seconds on the internet or for a lifetime in one-to-one engagements, learning to build an *Ideal Client Experience* is the beginning of your new success. You must systematize empathy. You must require that your entire team learn, get excited, and get on board. Ultimately, your whole company will begin to circle around this growth axiom:

It has never been about us.
It has always been about them.

This final note does lead us to a couple questions we did not have time to cover in this short read. Do you know who your ideal clients are? Do you have a singular, clear profile of that client that makes you smile when you win them and get to enjoy them as loyal customers? It is critically important that you learn how to distill your present client list down to your best clients. You must create an ideal client profile. Well, maybe that will be the subject of my next book.

Here is what some others are saying about the *Ideal Client Experience*:

H.B. introduced us to growing from the center instead of growing from the edges. This was all about strategic relationship building with the donors we were already in relationship with. As a result, in one fundraising event alone, we cut our budget by 75% and doubled our donations! (W. D. Development Director, Christian nonprofit)

I had learned almost everything you could learn about sales and marketing in my industry. When I began to use the Ideal Client Experience model in my advisory practice, not only were my clients impressed, but my focus on winning new, better clients has gone through the roof, and my team is getting onboard! (N.J. Financial Services)

My great concern was not about attracting new clients. Fact is, we have too many. My issue was learning to build a team that could work together and take care of the clients we already had. The Ideal Client Experience process has helped us conquer problems we thought we might never overcome. (S.T. Brand Enterprise)

One final question: In view of the clients you love, how long can you afford to wait?

I bet it is not very long.

Better get started.

NEED HELP?

Next steps.

Uncertain of what to do next? Do you have some unanswered questions at this point?

I will not leave you alone.

Call me. Seriously. My phone number is 719-633-2515. I am here to help.

I also designed an online course to help you power through some of your questions. It will help you build your own *Ideal Client Experience*. It includes self-paced learning, exercises, videos, and even some one-to-one conversations with your very own Growth Advocate℠.

Use the coupon code **MYICX** to gain free access to the course. On me. Enjoy.

The online course designed to help you make progress building your Ideal Client Experience!

ENDNOTES

Limited use of quotes and references are for inspiration only, used to illustrate, are credited generously, and are all considered fair use. Please enjoy this informally formatted list of resources quoted throughout this book.

- https://www.corp-intl.com/news/newsitem.aspx?ID=315
- PWC Consumer Intelligence Report. https://www.pwc.com/us/en/services/consulting/library/consumer-intelligence-series/future-of-customer-experience.html
- A Walker study titled, Customers 2020 cited by https://marketingdesks.com/ideal-customer-experience
- Gartner study titled Key Findings From the Gartner Customer Experience Survey cited SuperOffice https://www.superoffice.com/blog/customer-experience-statistics/
- Forrest Research data cited by https://www.webmarketingpros.com/how-customer-loyalty-drives-profitability/

- https://www.peoplekeep.com/blog/Employee-Retention-The-Real-Cost-of-Losing-an-Employee
- Nielsen https://www.nielsen.com/insights/2015/global-trust-in-advertising/ cited at https://www.themuse.com/advice/why-having-friends-at-work-is-actually-crucial-to-your-success
- The Loyalty Effect: The Hidden Force Behind Growth, Profits, and Lasting Value, Frederick F. Reichfeld.
- RedPointGlobal, https://www.redpointglobal.com/resources/addressing-the-gaps-in-customer-experience/
- https://www.forrester.com/report/Customer-Experience-Drives-Revenue-Growth-In-Europe-Too/RES130824
- MYCUSTOMER's 2018 customer journey mapping research report is based on a global survey of 248 customer experience professionals across EMEA, North America and Asia-Pacific. www.mycustomer.com Produced in conjunction with Quadient. https://www.quadient.com/resources

Recommended Resources

- https://walkerinfo.com/cxleader/customers-2020-a-progress-report/
- https://www.revenuegrowthengine.com/blog
- https://www.pwc.com/us/en/advisory-services/publications/consumer-intelligence-series/pwc-consumer-intelligence-series-customer-experience.pdf
- https://www.mckinsey.com/business-functions/operations/our-insights/the-ceo-guide-to-customer-

experience
- https://www.quadient.com/blog/customer-journey-map
- https://www.retailcustomerexperience.com/blogs/why-personalization-is-key-for-retail-customer-experiences/
- https://www.invespcro.com/blog/great-customer-experience/
- https://emplifi.io/resources/blog/customer-experience-statistics
- https://go.emplifi.io/us-uk-customer-expectations-report.html
- https://www.accenture.com/_acnmedia/PDF-77/Accenture-Pulse-Survey.pdf
- https://www.gartner.com/en/marketing/insights/articles/three-key-gartner-marketing-predictions-2021
- https://www.superoffice.com/blog/customer-experience-strategy/
- https://www.cpsa.com/resources/articles/the-link-between-loyalty-and-profitability
- https://officevibe.com/blog/infographic-friends-at-work
- https://www.gartner.com/en/marketing/insights/articles/key-findings-from-the-gartner-customer-experience-survey
- https://hbr.org/1996/03/learning-from-customer-defections
- https://www.mycustomer.com/resources/empathy-in-customer-service-a-consumer-survey
- https://www.researchgate.net/publication/242345850_Loyalty_as_a_philosophy_and_strategy_An_in

terview_with_Frederick_F_Reichheld
- https://inmoment.com/resource/2021-digital-customer-experience-trends-report/

ABOUT THE AUTHOR

H.B. Pasley

H.B. Pasley has been a coach, a creative, and a professional communicator for close to four decades. He has published many books and countless leadership guides, facilitated thousands of people in leadership development retreats, and has produced millions and millions of song streams over the years. Even after all that, he is fond of deflecting attention from his accomplishments by saying, "My real claim to fame is that I have failed at more ventures than most will ever attempt ... and I took a lot of notes."

He has founded works in tech, financial services, charitable orgs, and in the arts. He founded and presided over an arts-focused Christian nonprofit that for two decades served marginalized people. His DNA is to start things; however, it may be his lifelong work with very strong and talented people that has uniquely equipped him to be a professional advisor. It was "in the school of hard knocks," he says, where he gleaned his best wisdom for helping others. Refreshingly, H.B. openly speaks of his own failures as some of his greatest learning moments. He is a Growth Advocate℠ for business leaders. He helps people-first owners who are hitting their heads on growth problems.

Presently, H.B. lives in Colorado Springs, Colorado with his wife Robin, an award-winning interior designer. His two sons live in Phoenix, Arizona. H.B. loves golf, though he is bad at it. He is better at fly fishing, reading books, and hiking. He loves to be on the water.

www.idealclientexperience.com

P.S. Hey, want to be an author? Interested in publishing your own book? H.B. has two publishing partners to recommend that can help you accomplish your dreams in less time and for less money than you may have previously thought possible. Drop him a note at hbpasley@idealclientexperience.com.

www.neverdroptheballagain.com